The Butterfly's Guide To Haiku

Melissa Dolber Grappone
Don Foxe

donfoxe.com

CABALLUS
PRESS™

Copyright © 2018 don foxe

Printed in the United States of America

ISBN: 978-1-7321036-7-2

Written by Melissa Dolber Grappone and Don Foxe.
donfoxe.com

Produced by Caballus Press, North American Division
www.caballuspress.com

Stock images are used for illustrative purposes only.
Some stock imagery from Pixabay.com, Unsplach.com, and Pexels.com
Images on cover used with permission.

Acknowledgements

The Butterfly Effect Project [www.bepgirls.org] mission is *To empower, enlighten and enhance every girl's future; encouraging one girl at a time by eliminating one obstacle at a time.*

The project began March 8, 2014 with eight girls. Two-hundred-eight girls from the Long Island, NY area are now enrolled. Founded by Tijuana Fulford in an effort to offer a totally free program to empower girls by providing the tools to achieve emotional stability and self-confidence. The ultimate goals is for *bepgirls* to become a generation of women who are strong, independent, and knowledgable.

Donations and volunteers are encouraged. Discover more about bepgirls, how you can be part of the Project, and see the progress being made at www.bepgirls.org.

The Butterly's Guide To Haiku is being used by bepgirls to expand their knowledge and provide one more tool to empower their creativity.

American Portfolios Financial Services, Inc. (AP), a company with a history of community involvement, covered the costs associated with production and delivery of **The Butterfly's Guide To Haiku** to the girls at The Butterfly Effect Project enrolled in this haiku literary education venture.

The New York-based corporation encourages those who are a part of AP all across the nation to extend the commitment to service provided for its investment professionals and their clients into the local communities in which they live and work. By developing a culture that benefits all, AP strives to strengthen the ties which bind us together.

Smiles, laughter, and hope

   enrich everyone when led

      by a servant's heart. (AP)

Web Site and Social Media Addresses:
Web Site: americanportfolios.com
Facebook: @americanportfoliosapfs
Twitter: @APFS0901
LinkedIn: https://www.linkedin.com/company/american-portfolios/

Photo courtesy of AP and BEPgirls.

Konnichiwa (Good Day)

Ever have a problem expressing yourself? Worse, making someone understand what you are feeling when you can't seem to put those feelings into words!

Poetry helps. When you hear a song and it moves you, the lyrics are poetry. It isn't about rhyming or big words. It's about a writer sharing a feeling and a reader (or listener) getting it.

Haiku is a great way to learn about writing poetry because it can be very simple to learn. Just like learning to play a musical instrument. A few notes can become chords. Practice and you're soon playing songs.

As you progress, your haiku progresses.

Along the way you will see 🦋 . This means you're about to be given information you don't really need – history and culture lessons about haiku. Don't get worried about these details. They are just fun facts.

The first rule involves the structure of the poem.
A haiku poem consists of three lines.
    The first line contains five syllables;
        the second line contains seven syllables;
          the third line contains five syllables.

Kitsune is *fox* in Japanese. In Classical Japanese,
Kitsu-ne means *come and sleep*.

Haiku helps you become a better writer because you must place your thoughts into this strict format. Express yourself within the 5-7-5, but DO NOT ALLOW FRUSTRATION a place in your creativity.

In traditional haiku the look of the finished poem was nearly as important as the message. The Japanese use characters instead of an alphabet. Character-style writing lends itself to a more artistic-looking final product.

The majority of Japanese words are much shorter, containing fewer syllables than English. A Japanese haiku poet will find it easier to express themselves because they have more descriptive (short) words available.

For your ryokō (journey) we have designed this haiku handbook for the poet-writer using english. It will take you through the process of completing a haiku poem using what we consider the important aspects of haiku. You will discover how haiku lends itself to improving your ability to create a word picture. You will also be challenged to produce poetry that causes an emotional response from the reader.

You will discover how descriptions allow a reader to "see" what you see and "feel" what you do.

Your haiku handbook will walk you through simple steps to help you capture the spirit of nature. It is a guide to show you how to connect with others through words.

Once you understand how words can create feelings, capturing the spirit of haiku opens a world of allegory. That step requires another guide.

For the person seeking a place of calmness in this hectic, loud civilization we live in, haiku is an island of peace. The more you strive to integrate the many traits of haiku into your creation, the greater your sense of serenity. It is escapism in the purest form.

And it keeps you healthy. The creative process, combined with forcing your writing into a structured format stimulates the parts of your brain important to the prevention of dementia. Haiku is learning to dance with words. When you write a poem, you lead. When you read haiku, you follow.

Kotodama is the belief that mystical powers dwell in words and names. This belief is held by many cultures around the world. Spells, incantations, prayers, and chants are all proof of our belief in the power of language.

Fūjin (風神)

The Japanese Spirit of the Wind is a scary looking dude, but always depicted with a big grin. Read as if the wind blows the poem across you. Allow your smile to warm the words.

Fujin

To help get you started, Melissa has included twenty-six original haiku poems never before published. You can use these as examples,
or, in the spirit of Haiku Exchanges,
you can respond to any of her haiku with one of your own.

Notice Melissa changes the indents on some of her lines. This is done to give her haiku a certain look that feels right with the words. It is sometimes used to emphasize a line or make sure two items (thoughts; images; feelings) are connected. Whether you keep your haiku aligned or indent is your choice.

When you read, ask yourself:
    Do I feel a season of the year?
    Which senses do I experience when I read? [see, hear, feel, smell, taste]
    Is there an emotion Melissa felt that I understand?
    Is there a different emotion I feel?

    What do I think the poet was **writing** about (reality)?
    What do I think the poet was **thinking** about (the spirit of the words)?

Don Foxe   狐

Natsukashii (Happy Remembrance)

In a younger day with fewer pressures and more idle time, I filled endless hours and solitary moments lost in (and consoled by) nature. Perhaps that explains the appeal of haiku for me today.

I was introduced to the Japanese form of poetry in middle school where the rules were lax with the exception of one: 5-7-5 syllables on three lines. As long as we stuck to that construct there was free reign to create a haiku on anything we wanted.

Here is what I wrote:

> Love can bring one jewels.
> And yet, my love amounts to
>   cleaning the kitchen.

Much to my surprise, it was published in the school's literary magazine. I drew from the thoughts of the day weighing heavily on me – the care and concern for my mother who, at age forty-five, took a fall and broke her hip. I believe the heartfelt nature of my poem compelled the editor to make it one of the selections.

Conforming today to the traditional rules surrounding nature and the seasons, my haiku poems still remain personal. Inspired by the natural world around me to express the essence of someone in the present or from the past, I am comforted in the belief all things living now or at any other time are connected through the spirit of nature. It is this connectivity through haiku by which time is endless and moments less fleeting.

Recently, I reworked the poem about my mother from years ago. Using more of the basic rules of Haiku by tying it to nature and the seasons, here is how I transformed it:

> Cached in emerald
>   saplings give back carbon love
>   to a mother tree.

You are a young spirit imbued with the gifts of an open, unfiltered, and imaginative mind. As one grows older, the rigors of life can dull that. Haiku helped to restore my youthful sense of wonder. I look beyond whatever is around me to see something marvelous; something to appreciate and express through my own mind's eye.

I look forward to time spent creating and exchanging haiku with you. We all have the power to inspire those around us. Through haiku, the spirit waiting within you can be released. Your poetry will become part of your life's memorial. Your inspirations for all to hear and read.

Melissa Grappone

Haiku by Melissa

Early morning sun
   pushes softly through warm haze
      blushing radiance.

Daylight hours wane.
Ripe with promise, a late bloom
   holds before the storms.

Calm breeze parts jeweled wings
   from thistle; Painted Lady
         hailed the garden queen.

Golden light filters
through tree limbs of an orchard
ripening red pommes.

Buteo wings fanned
   catch thermals high off rock mounts
      gracing blue skies south.

Arid winds rising
      whisk sands - choking, stifling all
but a Desert Rose.

Gold-touched War Eagle;
    her wings open, talons lift
        soaring to the sun.

Sun's gaze waxes cold,
yet days inch longer, warmer,
bright with white-stretched rays.

Night breathes cold, shallow
      sleeping still, silent, dormant
            in endless grey time.

    Burrowed are toad and hare
as a swift cold front clips land
in the bitter morn.

     Frozen end of night,
an ice moon melts in the arms
              of a naked oak.

Photo by Melissa Grappone

Cloaked in canyon hue,
  nested, a wistful osprey
    awaits her return.

Twilight yields softly
  to harvest's last light, breathless
    over hushed hayfields.

Moist from melt the land
fills in with new born color
  Artful Earthliness!

Fire and ice feed
  living rock, foss spray, binding
    young-natured spirits.

Shadows on salt marsh
  rouse a gangling heron to
    air-bound artistry.

In hollowed darkness
  a hornbill longs for new life
    as all earth mums do.

Photo by Melissa Grappone

Full-hearted in songs
of day, a brown-eyed Robin
        "Peek-Tuts" time away.

Flitting colours hatched
  wept gold, gushed blue, tickled pink
    in butterfly dance.

Palmetto sways to
day's hot breath, charged with thunder
in the land of palms.

Day breaks late; gazing
eastward, a space trekker burns
red holes through the night.

New born light breaks through
the edge of day, arriving
in breath-taking awe.

Shaken from bay's breeze
bumbles cling to nectar 'for
the lavender's plucked.

From its core onto
    pathways flows the richness and
        beauty of a gem.

Precious daylight shines
    on glittered wings drenched with warmth
from a parting sun.

Tangerine mornings
        bid farewell to still shores with
            bittersweet kisses.

Part 1: The Basics

There are seventeen total syllables available to work with.

First Line = Five Syllables
Second Line = Seven Syllables
Third Line = Five Syllables

A syllable is a part of a word you pronounce as a unit. It is comprised of two speech sounds -- a vowel alone or a vowel with one or more consonants. The word *vowel* has two syllables: vow - el. The word *consonants* contains three syllables: con-so-nants.

BLUE SKY, LAYERED LEAVES
   contains five syllables and is an example of a first line.

Before worrying over the number of syllables, or how to divide words into lines containing the requisite number of sounds, you need to rediscover the world around you.

Without trying to be poetic, describe something you've seen that moved you enough that it remains a vivid image in your mind.

Example: Sitting on my patio, I looked up, my eye attracted to the way the blue sky mixed with the slender green leaves of the Saga Palm in my backyard. The wind brushed the leaves across the blue, giving me a peaceful moment following several days of turmoil.

Blue sky, layered leaves.
What about you? Write it here, or start your own journal.

The fun begins with the realization some moment in time actually touched you. If it happened once, it has happened before. It will occur again . . . especially when you are open to the experience.

Haiku engages the senses. In my example: sight. You also have touch, smell, hearing, taste, and a sixth sense — mystic. Some people experience things beyond the normal senses, and they have every right to share those.

Part 2: The Spirit of Haiku

The Seasons of the Year

In haiku you place the spirit of a season within your poem, trying not to actually name the time of year. For the moment, if you need to write out the season, do it. We will explore ways of changing it later.

In the example shown, BLUE SKY could mean spring or summer; possibly a crisp winter day; maybe a sad autumn moment. The spirit will be determined by the remaining words — I hope.

Haiku written in Japanese is much easier to accomplish than for english writers. Japanese has many more one-syllable words with deeper meanings connected to the words. It is also the poetry most connected to the culture, so over centuries certain words and colors have become accepted as having specific intentions.

Colors evoke images that relate to seasons such as white for snow, or grey for overcast, dreary days. Green often makes you think of spring, as do most pastel colors. Summer is usually thought of as vibrant blues, yellows and reds. Browns and orange tints create images of leaves changing ... autumn.

If you continue to explore your personal haiku, over time you will create your own pallet of words -- your words which represent your view of the universe.

With each of the seasons, write down words that make you think of that season when you read or hear them.

SPRING:

SUMMER:

FALL:

WINTER:

I Bet you ran out of space! Use a blank page and write more, or, as I hinted before, start a journal. A journal does not have to be dedicated to your haiku. You can write many things, and not like a diary, which often concerns personal interactions and feelings, a journal is more about your observations of the world.

Funny thing about language - it is personal. You may describe something that reminds you of summer; someone reads it and they get a wintry feeling. Ever wonder why arguments begin? Remember this. What you say and what they hear are not always the same thing.

Part 3: From You

What you see (or something that occurs) should be presented as **an image of your feelings** at the time you experienced the event. The best haiku are simple images. No metaphors and no elegant descriptions.

This is difficult and takes many attempts.

A metaphor is a term or phrase used to make a comparison between two things that are not alike but have something in common.

The snow is a white blanket - as in white snow covering the ground the way a white blanket covers your bed.

The classroom was a zoo – to describe students talking, moving around, laughing, working and making the room similar to the noise and activity of animals at a zoo.

Metaphors are great ways to describe things, but not to be overused in haiku.

Instead of the snow is a white blanket, you might write: *white icy blanket.* Hey, look at that -- five syllables.
Did it make you think of cold winter snow?

An *elegant description* is a fancy way of saying *fancy*. Some writers are very good at long, detailed descriptions that allow you to see what they see. Haiku poetry tries to do the same thing with simplicity. Fewer words; more emotions. Emotions create images, just as images bring on emotions.

First, write the vision. Perhaps a redbird singing while resting on a branch of a tree. Was the tree in bloom? Were the leaves fully formed? Did the vision of the bird or its song create the strongest impression? What did you feel?

Don't worry about haiku form. Write as little or as much as you remember.

This haiku began as I sat at my computer working on a book. My desk sits beside a window. I noticed a cardinal perched on a limb of the tree. The red feathers bright against the deep green leaves of the tree. A breeze moved the leaves, but was not strong enough to shake the branch or ruffle the bird. The cardinal chirped a few notes, and took flight.

Those ten seconds of escape from work made me realize how nice the early summer day outside appeared. I left my writing and went outside to enjoy the weather. To enjoy my life.

Red feathers so bright
against rich green leaves a-sway.
A song of calling.

Now write something you see, or saw, that made you happy.

Let's put it into haiku form: (**DO NOT WORRY** about being a wordsmith. Just create three lines of 5 - 7 – 5)

(5)

(7)

(5)

You may need to rewrite it several times. Getting a haiku right the first time is difficult for life-long poets. The fun is working through the process. It is why the best haiku collections often contain only a few poems.

You may stop . . .

You have learned the basics of haiku. You can create a haiku, and you know to try to place it within a season of the year. You have captured the first spirit.

You can use colors. Use fewer words to describe something. Allow your feelings to be part of your haiku.

You should compose four haiku. One poem set within each season of the year.

These four haiku will be sent to Melissa. She will send you a personal reply as to what she thinks of your work—an honest appraisal.

You will have a choice: make changes to your haiku based on her suggestions, or leave any or all of them as is.

If you would like to learn more about haiku, your workbook will continue to guide your journey.

As in life, moving forward can be difficult. It is, however, always more rewarding.

Note to You From Don and Melissa: *You can write one, two, three or four haiku. You can set them in any or all seasons . . . or none. Whatever you wish to send, you decide. We will cherish (and reply) to the haiku you share with us.*

Part 4: For Your Reader

Does your haiku lift the spirit of the reader?

This is the second spirit: the **_intention_** of haiku.

The person reading your haiku does not have to see what you saw. They do not need to experience the same feelings. You are not attempting to force someone else to share your vision. You want them to feel richer for having read your haiku.

This is accomplished with sight, smell, touch, taste, sound, and even pain or motion. When we read something and we experience a sensation, we are connecting with another person's spirit. This connection causes your spirit to lighten, boosted by the awareness we share this world with others 'like' us.

In my haiku, I hope you saw the red and green, heard the redbird's song, felt the motion of the soft breeze, and wanted to join him outside. I hope you realized the bird's call was summer's call for me to set aside obligation for a moment.

Part 5: Work Time

With each sense listed, write down words or a description that makes that sense create a happy or sad moment.

SMELL: fresh-baked cookies. puppy-breath. cut grass. (or bad) dog poop. old shoes.

Those are my examples -- what are yours?

I suggest you use a separate piece of paper for each sense. You can start now building a collection of ideas for future haiku.

SIGHT:

SMELL:

TOUCH:

TASTE:

SOUND:

PAIN: (physical)

PAIN: (emotional)

MOTION:

COLD:

WARM/HOT:

COMFORT:

SURPRISE:

17

"In achieving the smallest victory over an unbeatable adversary, we learn impossible exists only in the mind of a person unwilling to try. Haiku trains you to see the world with all of your senses. Writing haiku frees your imagination. Imagination allows you to overcome any obstacle."

I know I can create my own path. I can be the example for others.

I can walk a path paved by others, content I travel a way that is true. Harmony does not make me a follower.

I can blaze a path away from a well-traveled route, reaching my destination while seeing new vistas. I can cut a new trail without casting aside others.

What I must not do is stand still. Stopping also block others from progressing. My action or lack of action effects more than me.

The victory found when your haiku creates a moment of emotion for someone else is a step forward. The joy you experience for having touched another soul is a leap.

Part 6: KOTODAMI

You have what you need, including your own spirit. Words and names have magic, but magic requires a magician if it is to be used properly.

Your pen is your wand. Make magic.

Your final product for this project is to compose a haiku of your spirit.
- For this you do not look to the world outside. You look to your vision of your future.
- Describe you (the future you) when you accomplish becoming the person (the spirit) you intend to be.

The words are the warmth
lighting images so real
you live my fiction.

This haiku began my career as a writer. It guides me now because it remains my future. To write in a way that allows a reader to enjoy the experiences, the adventures, the emotions of the characters in my stories. This is the spirit I wish to be.

This project is not about finding your spirit. It is about releasing it. Fly butterfly. The breeze from your wings will become a storm capable of changing lives.

Haiku by Don Foxe

@realisticpoetry on twitter will place a photo and ask for poets to write what they see. Here are three haiku examples.

Lifelines on the palm
of a tree arrive in Spring
unaware of fall.

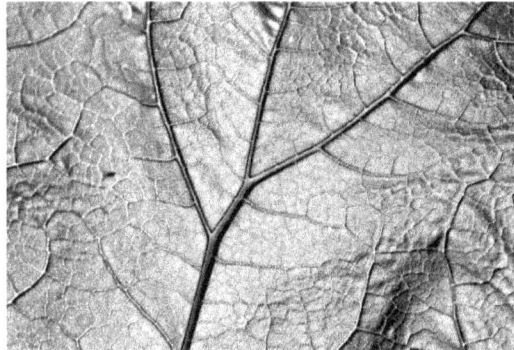

Hope. There's someone there.
Someone searching for the light
that leads them to me.

 I watch the night's storm
off shore, in the heat. I see
the storm watches back.

Exchanges are when you respond to a poem . . . the original need not be a haiku, and exchanges are not limited to haiku responses.

shellnjeff mcclendon
@ZanneQuinn

What of this day
I will remember most
is the way the clouds suddenly
covered the sun
and the light didn't stand a chance

My Response: @don_foxe

Days like this recall
light will shine above the clouds
and beyond the storm.

Melissa Dolber Grappone is a life-long resident of Long Island, N.Y. where she lives with husband, Gary. A corporate communications and marketing professional by trade, her creative interests have taken her to singing, accompanying her husband, and writing poetry. She is a graduate of the University of South Carolina, and received her Masters Degree from Hofstra University.

Her haiku compilations SEASONS OF HENKA SURU and HEIKU SEISHIN have been Amazon #1 in the Japanese/Haiku category and Top 100 in Poetry.

Don Foxe lives in Bluffton, S.C. with his wife Sarah, sharing a home with German Shepherds Risky and Dae. Don is the author of the science fiction series SPACE FLEET SAGAS, and the urban fantasy serial, DÚNMHARÚ.

PARANORMAL POETRY: A CHAPBOOK OF POEMS BY GHOSTS OF THE SOUTH CAROLINA LOWCOUNTRY is an Amazon Books #1 New Release and Top 100 in History/Short Stories.

donfoxe.com   @don_foxe

www.ingramcontent.com/pod-product-compliance
Lightning Source LLC
Chambersburg PA
CBHW080536030426
42337CB00023B/4765